# MOTHERS:
## A ROLE MODEL FOR PEACE

### DR. MUHAMMAD SALAH

**Published by:**

Unit No. E-10, 5 Jln SS 15/4G, Subang Square,
47500 Subang Jaya, Selangor, Malaysia
+603-5612-2407 (office) / +6017-399-7411 (mobile)
info@tertib.press
www.tertib.press
@tertibpress (Facebook & Instagram)

| | | |
|---|---|---|
| Author | : | Dr. Muhammad Salah |
| Transcriber & Editor | : | Norashikin Azizan |
| Cover design | : | Abdul Adzim Md Daim |
| Book design | : | Abdul Adzim Md Daim |


# MOTHERS: A ROLE MODEL FOR PEACE

First Edition: March 2023

# CONTENTS

# FOREWORD

*Mothers: A Role Model for Peace* is a collection of notes transcribed and adapted from a compelling lecture of the same title by Shaykh Dr. Muhammad Salah. In this lecture, the speaker draws upon Islamic teachings and stories from Islamic history to highlight the critical role that mothers play in creating a peaceful society.

As you journey through the pages of this book, you will discover the profound wisdom and guidance of the Qur'an and the teachings of the Prophet Muhammad (s.a.w.) on the importance of motherhood. You will be introduced to the stories of the mothers of the believers and other notable women in Islamic history, who serve as inspiring examples of the impact that mothers can have on society.

Shaykh Dr. Muhammad Salah emphasises the need for mothers to be recognised and supported in their role as primary caregivers and educators of their children. He highlights the unique abilities and strengths that mothers possess, including their nurturing instincts, compassion, and ability to instil values of peace and empathy in their children.

Through his insightful analysis and passionate call to action, Shaykh Dr. Muhammad Salah challenges us to recognise the transformative potential of motherhood and to honour and respect the vital role that mothers play in shaping the future of our societies.

Ultimately, *Mothers: A Role Model for Peace* is a powerful and inspiring book that draws upon Islamic teachings and history to shed light on the critical role of mothers in creating a more peaceful and just society. This book is a must-read for anyone interested in gaining a better understanding of the importance of motherhood in Islamic teachings and the impact that mothers can have on the world around them.

**Tertib Publishing**

# INTRODUCTION

We praise Allah and Allah alone and seek His help, and whomever Allah guides is the truly guided one and praise and blessings upon the Prophet (s.a.w.).

My brothers and sisters, may Allah teach us what we do not know and help us to act upon what we learned. *Āmīn.*

In the sound *ḥadith*, which is collected by Imam at-Tirmidhi, Imam al-Bukhari in al-Adab al-Mufrad and others and it is narrated by the great companion, Abu Hurayrah (r.a.):

The Prophet (s.a.w.) says:

"Whenever the servant of Allah dies, all his deeds will come to an end except from three ways: a continuous charity, a useful knowledge that he left behind or a righteous child will pray for him or her."

Sunan an-Nasa'i 3651

This is our subject of conversation. This is our investment in this life. We come, we learn and all we leave behind is a continuation of ourselves. A good offspring will remember us in their supplications and will benefit us when all our good deeds will end due to death. That is why among the supplications of the servant of The Merciful in Surah al-Furqan, Allah (s.w.t.) counted among the traits of *Ibadurrahman*:

$$\text{وَٱلَّذِينَ يَقُولُونَ رَبَّنَا هَبْ لَنَا مِنْ أَزْوَٰجِنَا وَذُرِّيَّـٰتِنَا قُرَّةَ أَعْيُنٍ وَٱجْعَلْنَا لِلْمُتَّقِينَ إِمَامًا ٧٤}$$

And those who say, "Our Lord, grant us from among our wives and offspring comfort to our eyes and make us a leader [i.e., example] for the righteous."

Surah al-Furqan: 74

This is the invocation; the connascent *du'a'* of *Ibadurrahman*. Lend us from our spouses and offspring—comfort to the eyes, ease to our minds and make us leaders for the righteous ones. Look at the high ambition. Not just make us righteous; not just make our children righteous, now, make us and our offspring leaders for the righteous. The biggest gain ever is whenever we settle in Paradise, *inshā'Allāh*, safely and enjoy the company of those whom we love especially our family members, our beloved spouses, parents and children.

# UNDERSTANDING THE ROLE OF A MOTHER

## Honour and Respect is A Two-Way Street

وَٱلَّذِينَ ءَامَنُوا۟ وَٱتَّبَعَتْهُمْ ذُرِّيَّتُهُم بِإِيمَـٰنٍ أَلْحَقْنَا بِهِمْ ذُرِّيَّتَهُمْ وَمَآ أَلَتْنَـٰهُم مِّنْ عَمَلِهِم مِّن شَىْءٍ ۚ كُلُّ ٱمْرِئٍ بِمَا كَسَبَ رَهِينٌ ۝

And those who believed and whose descendants followed them in faith—We will join with them their descendants, and We will not deprive them of anything of their deeds. Every person, for what he earned, is retained.

Surah aṭ-Ṭur: 21

In Surah aṭ-Ṭur, Allah (s.w.t.) delivers the glad tidings for those who believed and did good and righteous deeds—they will make it to heaven and Allah will come for their eyes by making their offspring follow their footsteps in the *dunya* and make them join them in the *akhirah*. This is indeed the ultimate success—to enjoy the company of your beloved ones, your children, and your offspring in *Jannah*. May Allah grant us this honour. For this reason, Islam cares a lot about raising children and that begins very early—from the moment you decide to get married. Once, a man came to 'Umar ibn Khaṭṭab (r.a.) to complain about his disobedient son. In the Qur'an, there are two instances where Allah (s.w.t.) declared that we have to worship Him and believe in the oneness of Him then commanded us to do good to our parents. First in Surah an-Nisa', verse 36:

وَٱعۡبُدُواْ ٱللَّهَ وَلَا تُشۡرِكُواْ بِهِۦ شَيۡـًٔاۖ وَبِٱلۡوَٰلِدَيۡنِ إِحۡسَٰنًا ... ﴿٣٦﴾

Worship Allah and associate nothing with Him, and to parents do good…

Surah an-Nisa':36

Then in Surah al-Isra', verse 23:

وَقَضَىٰ رَبُّكَ أَلَّا تَعۡبُدُوٓاْ إِلَّآ إِيَّاهُ وَبِٱلۡوَٰلِدَيۡنِ إِحۡسَٰنًاۚ إِمَّا يَبۡلُغَنَّ عِندَكَ ٱلۡكِبَرَ أَحَدُهُمَآ أَوۡ كِلَاهُمَا فَلَا تَقُل لَّهُمَآ أُفࣲّ وَلَا تَنۡهَرۡهُمَا وَقُل لَّهُمَا قَوۡلࣰا كَرِيمࣰا ﴿٢٣﴾

And your Lord has decreed that you worship not except Him, and to parents, good treatment.

Whether one or both of them reach old age [while] with you, say not to them [so much as], "uff", and do not repel them but speak to them a noble word.

Surah al- Isra':23

This is significant since Allah (s.w.t.) places our parents right after Him, implying the importance to be good and dutiful to your parents. Honour and respect your parents. There was one time, this man came to complain about his disobedient son to 'Umar ibn Khaṭṭab (r.a.). 'Umar ibn Khaṭṭab (r.a.) ordered that the son should be presented before him. When he showed up, he (r.a.) blamed him. He (r.a.) said, "How could you do that to your father? How could you be dishonouring and disrespecting your father?" The child said, "O' *Amirul Mu'minin*, don't the children have rights upon their parents too?" He (r.a.) said, "True." Then the child said, "Would you please inform me about the children's rights upon the parents?" So 'Umar (r.a.) said: "Number one: upon the father, it is his duty to choose an honourable and a good mother to bear his children. And he must give him a good name. Then to teach him the Qur'an." Then the boy said, "O' *Amirul Mu'minin*. My father has indeed deprived me of all those rights. He chose a dishonourable woman. He named me Ju'la (cockroach)."

Some people do choose deliberately awful names for their children by means of protection. They think that when they choose awful names, the children will live longer and be protected from the evil eye. This is a myth. "He named me Ju'la, what an awful name. When people call me, I feel ashamed of myself. And furthermore, he didn't teach me a word of the Qur'an. These are what my father did to me." So 'Umar ibn Khaṭṭab (r.a.) looked at the father and he said to him, "The ingratitude, the disrespect and dishonour came from you first. You dishonoured him in the first place, and this is the result. He's being disobedient to you."

# MOTHERS AS A SYMBOL OF PEACE

Normally, when we speak about peace, it is greatly and widely misunderstood that peace may mean weakness or submission or giving up due to weakness. While peace in the Qur'an and the *sunnah* does not mean that at all. Peace can only be achieved when you are strong, when you are powerful and when you are just, because there is no peace without justice. So, if somebody thinks that they can bring up their children in a peaceful and comfortable life while injustice has been practised at home, then it will stay as a dream that will never come true.

Raising children is the most important task and responsibility and it is laid on both parents' shoulders. But the one who plays the most important role in that, is no doubt, the mother. Mothers play a great role in building a generation. The better the mother is at raising her children, the more successful the *ummah* is built. You hardly see a great man except that a great woman is behind him—who left her traits in his personality, who left her fingerprint on his behaviour. Through the milk that she fed him and the womb which she provided him when he was young, the child gets affected by his mother as early as pregnancy, when he was just a foetus. That is why there is a list of do's and don'ts. A list of things a mother cannot do, cannot consume, cannot take—even to the extent of medications. Physicians and pharmacologists say that there is no safe medication during pregnancy. Despite the fact that some drugs—say—safe during the second or third trimester. The fact that there is no medication that is safe during pregnancy, let alone smoking, taking drugs, or narcotics, which will definitely lead to the malformation and deformity of the unborn child. Each pack of cigarettes—says on it— *'SMOKING CAUSES DEFORMITY ON THE CHILD'*. So the mother's behaviour, whether good or bad, will definitely affect the child. It will bring either peace and tranquillity or anxiety and depression to the child. It will make him either physically and emotionally healthy or sick and deformed. It is very interesting that the Qur'an covers this area particularly the emotional health of the mother which affects the emotional health of the child. Do you know that when the mother is happy with her pregnancy, that also affects the child positively? Versus whenever she is sad, for instance, in many cultures up until today, if the parents know that the baby is a girl, they will feel sad and sorrowful. That affects the embryo. That is why Allah (s.w.t.) said in Surah as-Shura 49-50, to come for the parents and assure them that it is all from Allah and He knows what is best for them.

لِّلَّهِ مُلْكُ ٱلسَّمَـٰوَٰتِ وَٱلْأَرْضِ ۚ يَخْلُقُ مَا يَشَآءُ ۚ يَهَبُ لِمَن يَشَآءُ إِنَـٰثًا وَيَهَبُ لِمَن يَشَآءُ ٱلذُّكُورَ ﴿٤٩﴾

To Allah belongs the dominion of the heavens and the earth; He creates what He wills. He gives to whom He wills female [children], and He gives to whom He wills males. (49)

أَوْ يُزَوِّجُهُمْ ذُكْرَانًا وَإِنَـٰثًا ۖ وَيَجْعَلُ مَن يَشَآءُ عَقِيمًا ۚ إِنَّهُۥ عَلِيمٌ قَدِيرٌ ﴿٥٠﴾

Or He makes them [both] males and females, and He renders whom He wills barren. Indeed, He is Knowing and Competent. (50)

Surah ash-Shura: 49-50

To Allah belongs the heaven and the earth and what is in them. He creates whatever He likes. He grants whomever He wills. Girls, boys. Up to Him. And He gives whomever He will both boys and girls. It is up to Him. There is no objection to Allah's will. Both parents should be pleased with whatever Allah (s.w.t.) provides for them. As far as childhood—once the child is born, he would be very much affected by his mother, the closest person to him—even closer to him than the father. The Qur'an says in Surah al-Baqarah verse 233:

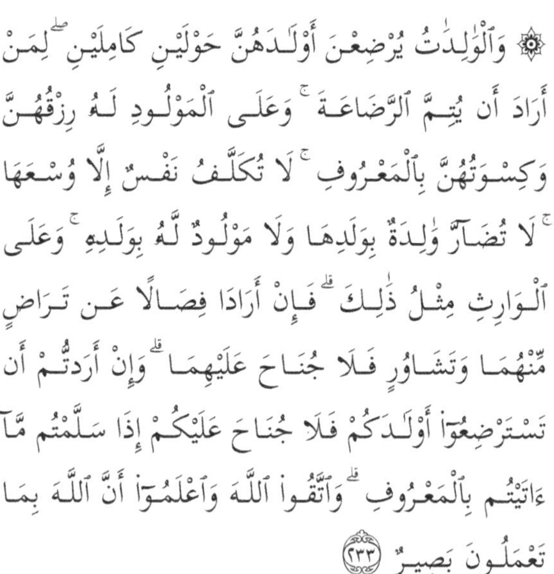

Mothers may nurse [i.e., breastfeed] their children two complete years for whoever wishes to complete the nursing [period]. Upon the father is their [i.e., the mothers'] provision and their clothing according to what is acceptable. No person is charged with more than his capacity. No mother should be harmed through her child, and no father through his child. And upon the [father's] heir is [a duty] like that [of the father]. And if they both desire weaning through mutual consent from both of them and consultation, there is no blame upon either of them. And if you wish to have your children nursed by a substitute, there is no blame upon you as long as you give payment according to what is acceptable. And fear Allah and know that Allah is Seeing of what you do.

The Qur'an recommended that the mothers should nurse and breastfeed their babies for two complete years. This is an ideal proposal. Breastfeed the child yourself, for two complete years. It is scientifically proven that breastfeeding promotes in both physical and emotional health. Guess what? Not only one way, not only the physical and emotional health of the child, but of the mother as well. So, both the mother and the child will maintain their physical and emotional health conditions simply due to breastfeeding or natural nursing. Studies show that breastfeeding mothers suffer less postpartum depression and anxiety than the formula-feeding mothers. The warmth of the hugs and kisses, changing the diaper for the child is a very special relation that instils a lot of feelings and emotions in the heart and the mind of the child. It is indeed an awful practice to handover the child when he is born to somebody else, whether it is a babysitter or a maid to take care of them. That does indeed disconnect the child from his mother, who should play the most important role in shaping his future. This is because it does not start later, nor does it stop at a certain age as mentioned earlier: it starts during pregnancy, and it does not end until the life itself ends. The Prophet (s.a.w.) has said in a sound *hadith* which was collected by Imam al-Bukhari:

حَدَّثَنَا إِسْمَاعِيلُ، حَدَّثَنِي مَالِكٌ، عَنْ عَبْدِ اللَّهِ بْنِ دِينَارٍ، عَنْ عَبْدِ اللَّهِ بْنِ عُمَرَ ـ رضى الله عنهما ـ أَنَّ رَسُولَ اللَّهِ صلى الله عليه وسلم قَالَ « أَلاَ كُلُّكُمْ رَاعٍ، وَكُلُّكُمْ مَسْئُولٌ عَنْ رَعِيَّتِهِ، فَالإِمَامُ الَّذِي عَلَى النَّاسِ رَاعٍ وَهْوَ مَسْئُولٌ عَنْ رَعِيَّتِهِ، وَالرَّجُلُ رَاعٍ عَلَى أَهْلِ بَيْتِهِ وَهْوَ مَسْئُولٌ عَنْ رَعِيَّتِهِ، وَالْمَرْأَةُ رَاعِيَةٌ عَلَى أَهْلِ بَيْتِ زَوْجِهَا وَوَلَدِهِ وَهِيَ مَسْئُولَةٌ عَنْهُمْ، وَعَبْدُ الرَّجُلِ رَاعٍ عَلَى مَالِ سَيِّدِهِ وَهْوَ مَسْئُولٌ عَنْهُ، أَلاَ فَكُلُّكُمْ رَاعٍ وَكُلُّكُمْ مَسْئُولٌ عَنْ رَعِيَّتِهِ ».

Narrated 'Abdullah bin 'Umar:

Allah's Messenger (s.a.w.) said, "Surely! Every one of you is a guardian and is responsible for his charges: The Imam (ruler) of the people is a guardian and is responsible for his subjects; a man is the guardian of his family (household) and is responsible for his subjects; a woman is the guardian of her husband's home and of his children and is responsible for them; and the slave of a man is a guardian of his master's property and is responsible for it. Surely, every one of you is a guardian and responsible for his charges."

Ṣaḥīḥ al-Bukhari 7138

أَلاَ كُلُّكُمْ رَاعٍ، وَكُلُّكُمْ مَسْئُولٌ عَنْ رَعِيَّتِهِ

Every one of you is a guardian. And every guardian will be held accountable and would be asked about those who are under his guardianship,

وَالْمَـرْأَةُ رَاعِيَةٌ عَلَى أَهْـلِ بَيْـتِ زَوْجِهَا وَوَلَـدِهِ وَهِـيَ مَسْـئُولَةٌ عَنْهُـمْ

And the mother too is a guardian of her household and should be asked and questioned during the Day of Judgement about her children and offspring. So, if the father's role is to put food and bread on the table; then the mother's role is to keep close ties and closeness to the child and to instil in him or her good traits and manners.

To further illustrate how this can be practical to all the mothers out there, we must explore the history of great women in Islam such as the stories of the mothers of the believers and other notable women.

# STORIES OF GREAT WOMEN IN ISLAM

Islam gives utmost respect and honour to women, regardless of their nationality or religious affiliation. Whether a woman is a daughter, wife, sister, or mother, she is highly regarded. It is crucial to focus on all aspects of a woman's life since today's daughter will be tomorrow's wife and mother. However, we will only discuss a few examples of Muslim women who serve as role models. The expected role of mothers is learned from historical figures such as Ummahatul Mu'minin and other noteworthy women in Islamic history.

## The mother of Nu'man ibn Bashir (r.a.)

Nu'man ibn Bashir (r.a.) was a great companion, and his parents were companions as well. He narrated a *hadith* that is agreed upon its authenticity. He said, "When I was a child, my father decided to give me *'atiyyah* (a valuable gift). But my mother objected, and she said, 'You have to consult the Prophet (s.a.w.) and have him witness to that.'" So, Nu'man's father went to the Prophet (s.a.w.) and said, "O' Rasulullah, I was planning to give Nu'man a gift. But my wife said that I have to get you to witness it." Then the Prophet (s.a.w.) asked him, "Do you have any other children besides him?" He said, "Yes." Look where the mother was coming from. So, the Prophet's (s.a.w.) second question was, "Did you give each and every one of them *'atiyyah*, that is similar to what you are going to give Nu'man?" He said, "No." Then, the Prophet (s.a.w.) objected to that and he said,

$$\text{" فَاتَّقُوا اللَّهَ، وَاعْدِلُوا بَيْنَ أَوْلَادِكُم "}$$

Fear Allah pertaining to your children and treat them justly.

This narration can be found in the collection of Imam al-Bukhari *hadith* number 2587.

Fear Allah pertaining to your children and treat them justly. Be fair to them. If you give one child a valuable thing, you have to give the others as well. You must treat them justly. This is basically what causes discord, disunity, and hatred between the members of the same family. In many cases, it happens because the father prefers one of his sons, or a son over a daughter, or one of the children by extra-giving to one, depriving the others, or giving the boys more than the girls and so on. That eliminates the peace and tranquillity from society and leaves the children until death to be hating and refusing to talk to each other. Why? Because of this misdoing and injustice of one of the parents. It could be the father or the mother. So, look at the behaviour of 'Amrah bint Rawaḥah—Umm Nu'man ibn Bashir and her pearls of wisdom. Even in normal cases, situations like this will make a mother happy, especially when she is a co-wife, and the father only gives her son something that he would not give the others. Rather, she would encourage him to do that for her son. But not for Umm Nu'man ibn Bashir.

# Umm Salamah (r.a.)

Umm Salamah (r.a.) or Hind bint Abi Umayya was a companion of the Prophet (s.a.w.) during the Treaty of Hudaybiyyah. It is crucial to understand the context surrounding the treaty, as it took place during a significant time in Islamic history. The treaty was signed in the 6th year of *hijrah* after the Muslims had already engaged in major battles against the Quraysh. Despite not having conquered Makkah yet, the Muslims had established themselves as a powerful force in Madinah. Following their victories in battles such as Badr, Uḥud, Khandaq and Aḥzab, the Muslims found themselves in a position of power and authority that they had not experienced before. Despite this newfound power, the Muslims had been unable to make the sacred pilgrimage to Makkah, something that weighed heavily on their hearts, especially that of the Prophet. They longed to witness the Kaʿbah once again with their own eyes and to perform *ḥajj* and *ʿumrah* in complete devotion to Allah.

One morning, the Prophet (s.a.w.) woke up with a radiant face, brimming with happiness. He just had a dream, which was a form of revelation that his companions were completing their pilgrimage, having shaved their heads, and emerged from the state of *iḥram.* He knew that this dream would come true, as all the dreams of Prophets are divinely inspired. In response to this revelation, over a thousand companions, both male and female gathered with their sacrificial animals, and unarmed according to the laws of *iḥram*. They proceeded towards Makkah, which was still considered an enemy territory at that time. The companions were elated and overjoyed to fulfill their longing of going to Makkah.

It was impossible to conceal or go unnoticed with a caravan as large as theirs, and once the Quraysh became aware of their plans, they dispatched a military unit to intercept them. However, the Prophet (s.a.w.) changed course and attempted to enter through a different route, leading the entire Muslim congregation to the plains of Hudaybiyyah. While they were there, the camel the Prophet was riding, known as al-Qaswa', suddenly halted, knelt, and refused to move any further. Despite their best efforts, the Prophet and his companions were unable to coax the camel into continuing their journey.

At that point, the Prophet came to the realisation that there was a deeper reason for his camel's refusal to move, beyond just mere exhaustion. He explained to his companions that the same Divine Force that prevented the elephants from entering Makkah was now preventing his camel, al-Qaswa', from moving forward.

After the Muslims arrived at Hudaybiyyah, tensions between them and the Quraysh escalated. The Makkans became convinced that the Muslims were preparing to attack them, and in response, they sent another delegation to negotiate with the Muslims. 'Uthman ibn 'Affan was sent back with the delegation to explain the situation and attempt to negotiate an agreement. However, as events unfolded, the situation became increasingly fraught. Finally, the Prophet (s.a.w.) and the leaders of Quraysh began to negotiate the terms of the Muslims' entry into Makkah.

The arrogance of the Quraysh was evident in their first condition: the Muslims were to immediately return to Madinah without ever setting foot in Makkah. Even if they were allowed to return the following year, they were only permitted to stay for three days. These conditions devastated the Muslims who had sacrificed so much and had hoped to fulfill the dream of the Prophet and experience the spiritual fulfillment of *'umrah*. Nevertheless, the Prophet (s.a.w.) agreed to the conditions imposed by the Quraysh, and the Treaty of Hudaybiyyah was signed.

Although the Prophet's heart was heavy, he understood that this was what was necessary. He then commanded his *sahabah* to sacrifice their animals and shave their heads, signifying the end of their *ihram* and the conclusion of their journey.

The Muslim community was experiencing unprecedented emotional turmoil, as they found themselves objecting to the actions of their beloved Messenger for the first time ever. This was a group of dedicated and early believers of Islam who were refusing to comply with his command, a situation that the Prophet (s.a.w.) had never encountered before. He was both saddened and upset so he (s.a.w.) sought solace in the tent of Umm Salamah.

Umm Salamah's wise advice to the Prophet Muhammad, to sacrifice his animal and shave his head, proved to be a pivotal moment in the history of the Muslim nation. Her understanding of the emotions and devotion of the *ṣaḥabah* allowed her to offer a simple yet powerful solution that prevented a potential disaster. Her words had a profound impact and helped to unite the community once again. It is a testament to her wisdom and insight as a respected figure within the early Muslim community.

When the Prophet (s.a.w.) emerged from his tent in silence, his companions watched in increasing humility and embarrassment as he sacrificed the animal and shaved his head. Overwhelmed by the realisation of their rebellion, and in grief that they had displeased their Messenger in such a severe manner, they immediately followed his lead, thus proving that Umm Salamah's words were truly that of a brilliant stateswoman, a wise adviser, and a wife who was able to support and assist her husband in the manner he needed most. Can you imagine what would happen to this *ummah* if Umm Salamah (r.a.) did not offer them her beautiful and wise advice?

## Umm al-Imam ash-Shafi'e (r.a.h.)

We all know al-Imam as-Shafi'e (r.a.h.). But do we know how he was deeply influenced by his mother? Often referred to as Shaykh al-Islam, as-Shafi'e was one of the four great Sunni imams, whose legacy on judicial matters and teaching eventually led to the formation of Shafi'e school of *fiqh*. He was born in Gaza, the same year as Imam Abu Hanifah (r.a.h.) passed away. Soon after he was born, his father passed away. So, he was an orphan. His mother, Fatimah binti Ubaidillah Azdiyah, with all her might, travelled to Makkah with her son in order to teach him the *din*. She managed to make him memorise the entire Qur'an at the age of seven and Muwatta' at ten. She worked hard to provide for him so that he could seek knowledge. After he memorised the Qur'an and the Muwatta', she sent him to join the Hudhayl tribe to perfect and master the Arabic language—which he did—and he became the reference of the Arabic language and grammar in the whole Arab world. Then he was chosen by Imam Malik to be his student. This mother, the whole *ummah* owes her this great favour. After all, a child's first *madrasah* is on the lap of the mother. Fatimah binti Ubaidillah proved this.

# The mother of Sufyan ath-Thawri (r.a.)

This is the story of an *Amirul Mu'minin* in *ḥadith* and his mother. He was a renowned scholar of *ḥadith* and *fiqh*. He was known for his exceptional memory and ability to narrate *ḥadith* with precision and accuracy. Like Imam al-Shafi'e, he was an orphan, and his mother was extremely poor. But she was so determined, and she had a high and great ambition: to make her son a great scholar. So, she said, "Son, you seek knowledge; and I will provide for you with the proceeds of my spinning wheel." She was weaving day and night to earn her living to suffice for her son to seek knowledge until we had finally an *Amirul Mu'minin* in the *ḥadith*: one of the greatest *muḥaddithin*, Sufyan ath-Thawri (r.a.).

# The mother of Hudhayfah ibn Yaman (r.a.)

One of the companions of the Prophet (s.a.w.) was known as The Keeper of the Secret of the Messenger of Allah. The Prophet (s.a.w.) trusted him with his secret, particularly with *al-Munafiqun*. At that time, Hudhayfah was commissioned to watch their movements and follow their activities. The hypocrites, because of their secrecy and intimate knowledge of the developments and plans of the Muslims, presented a greater threat to the community than external enemies. One day his mother asked him, "Dear son, when was the last time you saw the Prophet (s.a.w.)?" "Three days ago." "What? Three whole days? You didn't see the Prophet (s.a.w.)? How could you have the patience to stay away from the Prophet (s.a.w.) for three days?" This is when he got so close to the Prophet (s.a.w.) to the extent that he chose him to be أمين سر رسول الله or 'The Keeper of Secrets'.

# Umm Sulaym (r.a.)

The most knowledgeable *faqih* of Madinah, the city of the Prophet (s.a.w.) is Malik ibn Anas (r.a.). He was raised among both his parents, but the favour his mother had upon this *ummah* is not to be forgotten. At an early age, she made him memorise the Qur'an. He used to have a turban over his head and she ordered him to go to a great *faqih* and instructed him with the following. She said: "Son, learn from his *akhlaq, adab* and etiquette, before the knowledge." Before science comes the *shari'ah*. Because the Prophet (s.a.w.) said: "I have been sent exclusively to perfect good manners." (al-Adab al-Mufrad, Book 14 Ḥadith 273)

Talking about manners, it is indeed a common problem that some parents may verbally instruct their children to behave in a certain way, but they do not model that behaviour themselves. This inconsistency can confuse children and make it difficult for them to learn and adopt the desired behaviour. For example, if a parent tells their child to always tell the truth, but then lies to someone on the phone in front of the child, the child may become confused and unsure about what is expected of them.

It is important for parents to model the behaviour they want their children to exhibit, and to be consistent in their words and actions. If a parent wants their child to be honest, then they should also strive to be honest themselves, even in small ways. If a parent catches themselves acting in a way that contradicts what they are teaching their child, they can use it as an opportunity to explain to their child why they made a mistake and how they plan to correct it. This can help reinforce the importance of the desired behaviour and show the child that everyone makes mistakes, but it is important to take responsibility and make things right.

Therefore, parents should strive to be positive role models for their children and to teach and model good behaviour consistently. Not too many parents pay attention to this, but by studying the Prophet (s.a.w.), the mothers of the believers, the companions, and the great Muslim women who gave excellent examples and were role models for this *ummah*, we can learn. It is not necessarily that every mother will be wise enough to instruct her children to live a happy life and maintain this happiness afterwards. But everybody is required to see the necessary knowledge and gain the required experience to protect their families in order to fulfil the responsibility as stated in Ṣaḥīḥ al-Bukhari 7138:

"...Surely, every one of you is a guardian and responsible for his charges."

Back to the story of the mother of Anas ibn Malik. She was Umm Sulaym or Rumaysa bint Milhan (r.a.). For all the mothers, make it a point to study the biography of Umm Sulaym (r.a.). Ponder it, reflect upon it, and try to imitate it. To be a successful mother and a role model not just for your child, but for the upcoming generations, *inshā'Allāh*. Umm Sulaym accepted Islam first. Her husband, Malik ibn Nard did not. They had their only child, Anas, who was Anas ibn Malik (r.a.). He was young, around under ten years old. Every time he enters, she would teach him to say, '*Lā ilāha illallāh, Muḥammadar Rasūlullāh.*' The father got upset, so he left Madinah and went to Syam and died there. Once the Prophet (s.a.w.) arrived in Madinah and migrated there, she took her only son, Anas to the Prophet (s.a.w.) and she did him the best favour and the *ummah* a great favour. By sending Anas at this young age, she said, "O' Rasulullah, people are bringing gifts. I have nothing to bring, but please accept the service of my son. I want my son to be in your service." Well, he was not a maid. Rather, he was chosen by the Prophet (s.a.w.) to educate him, to teach him. So that afterwards Anas ibn Malik would narrate for us this great knowledge of the *akhlaq* and the *adab* which will help the *ummah* with the manners of the Prophet (s.a.w.). Anas ibn Malik—the Prophet (s.a.w.) once told him, "O' Anas, I want to send you to someplace, but do not tell anyone. Keep my secret." He said, "Certainly, O' Rasulullah." Because of that, he went home late. So, his mother asked, "Where have you been?

What took you so long?" He said, "Well, the Prophet (s.a.w.) sent me somewhere." She said, "Where?" He said, "I can't tell." Mind you, this is a child. "I cannot tell." "Why not?" "Because the Prophet (s.a.w.) said to keep this a secret." Look at the mother. Not acting out of curiosity, she did not investigate and said to Anas, "I'm your mother. Tell me, where did he send you now?" Instead, she said to her son, "Keep the Prophet's secret. Do not reveal it to anyone." This is how the Muslim mother brings the *akhlaq*, peace and tranquillity to her household, by being a role model.

One day, a person by the name of Abu Ṭalḥah came to propose to Umm Sulaym (r.a.). He was not a Muslim, but he was a wise man. She said, "O' Abu Talhah, if you want to marry me, my dowry should be your Islam." (Sunan an-Nasa'i 3340). That was the greatest and the most expensive dowry in the history of Islam. Abu Ṭalḥah married Umm Sulaym, the mother of Anas ibn Malik (r.a.) and the dowry was to accept Islam. Soon after they got married, they had a child. But the child was severely ill. So, Abu Ṭalḥah went to the *masjid*; went out for some business, and when he returned home, he asked about his son. He said, "How's our son?" She said, "He's very quiet. He feels very comfortable. He is much better than before." He said, "Fine." because he had company. She offered them dinner. They all ate and after the company or the guests left, she adorned herself and they went to sleep. And he had an intimate relationship with her. Then before Fajr and after he fulfilled his need, she said, "O' Abu Ṭalḥah, I have an inquiry." He said, "What is it?" She said, "O' Abu Ṭalḥah, if some people borrow something from another family and then (the members of the family) ask for its return, would they refuse to give it back to them?" He said, "No, that's not proper. It is an *amanah*." Then she said, "O' Abu Ṭalḥah, Allah has given us an *amanah*, and He called it back. He took our son." Abu Ṭalḥah (r.a.) was so upset. Not because his son died, but because when the son was in the other room, waiting for the burial, they had a relationship. So, he went to the Prophet (s.a.w.) to complain. The Prophet (s.a.w.) was so impressed with the behaviour of this wise and patient woman and how she handled it. He (s.a.w.) said, "May Allah bless the night you spent together!". Allah (s.w.t.) accepted the *du'a'* of the Prophet (s.a.w.). They had a beautiful child and he (s.a.w.) said, "When you have the child, do not touch him before I come." Then he (s.a.w.) made the *taḥnik* by himself to the child and prayed for him. (Combined narrations from Ṣaḥiḥ al-Bukhari 1301 & 5470, Ṣaḥiḥ Muslim 2144b, Musnad al-Tayalisi 2168, Musnad Ahmad 12210 & 14281 & Ṣaḥiḥ ibn Ḥibban 7188). From his offspring, they had ten children who memorised the Qur'an.

These are Umm Sulaym, Umm Salamah, the mother of Hudhayfah ibn Yaman and other many, many examples we have, brothers and sisters. Our problem is that we do not read. And if we read, we tend to forget. The *sahabah* did not memorise the whole Qur'an in just one sitting. It took 'Umar ibn Khattab almost 10 years to memorise Surah al-Baqarah. Why? Because he would take 10 verses by 10 verses. Memorising the Qur'an for the companions was not a big deal. It was their language. They had memorised tens of thousands of phrases of poetry. But their practice was that when they learned, they practised—they act upon the instructions of the *ayat*, then they memorise. This is the right setup. We have the most beautiful religion. As a matter of fact, it is the only valid religion.

إِنَّ ٱلدِّينَ عِندَ ٱللَّهِ ٱلْإِسْلَٰمُ ۗ ... ﴿١٩﴾

Indeed, the religion in the sight of Allah is Islam...

Surah Ali-'Imran: 19

And whatever Allah and His messenger (s.a.w.) prescribe for us is indeed the best way.

# REMINDERS FOR MOTHERS

Our primary objective is to establish a harmonious and contented atmosphere within our household by creating a family unit with our children. To accomplish this, there are three essential values and items that mothers must prioritise when imparting them to their children. By paying attention to these values, we aim to promote a peaceful state of mind and tranquillity in our household. The mother holds a pivotal role in ensuring that these values are instilled within the children and implemented in their daily lives. The successful implementation of these values will lead to a household that is characterised by happiness, peace, and serenity, creating an environment that is conducive to the well-being and growth of all family members.

# To practise vigilance

The three dimensions of our religion are *Islam, iman* and *iḥsan*. Simply put, Islam is outward submission to the will of Allah; *iman* is actualising our faith and submission and *iḥsan* is doing our best in Islam—achieving spiritual excellence. *Iḥsan* is indeed the highest level of our religious practice and this is when the concept of *al-muraqabah* or vigilance is manifested. Through *muraqabah,* a person watches over their heart and soul—they are aware that Allah is watching them and is with them at all times.

I visited some people at their house once when their son was in high school. At that time, he was studying by himself in a room. Then, I saw a beautiful sign that was hung against the wall. They wrote in handwriting for him, "Son, you are not alone." That was it. If you are by yourself in a room, you are indeed not alone. Allah (s.w.t.) is with you. That means a lot, and that explains a lot. Then, *taqwa*—wherever you are—the awareness of Allah's presence, whether in private or in public, before the parents, or at school. Those who live in the West are confronted with the biggest challenge, which is the family at home love to live an Islamic life in many cases, but unfortunately, when the kids go to school, particularly in public school, they are different. That is why the children tend to carry their masks with them all the time. The mask would only be worn at home because their normal behaviour will be however they behave at school. So, the girl, for example, when she steps out of the house, will take off the hijab and the son will hang around with negative people. Nothing can treat this except instilling the concept of the awareness of Allah's presence at all times and in all places.

# To prefer others over oneself

وَٱلَّذِينَ تَبَوَّءُو ٱلدَّارَ وَٱلْإِيمَٰنَ مِن قَبْلِهِمْ يُحِبُّونَ مَنْ هَاجَرَ إِلَيْهِمْ وَلَا يَجِدُونَ فِى صُدُورِهِمْ حَاجَةً مِّمَّآ أُوتُوا۟ **وَيُؤْثِرُونَ** عَلَىٰٓ أَنفُسِهِمْ وَلَوْ كَانَ بِهِمْ خَصَاصَةٌ ۚ وَمَن يُوقَ شُحَّ نَفْسِهِ فَأُو۟لَٰٓئِكَ هُمُ ٱلْمُفْلِحُونَ ﴿٩﴾

*And [also for] those who were settled in the Home [i.e., al-Madinah] and [adopted] the faith before them. They love those who emigrated to them and find not any want in their breasts of what they [i.e., the emigrants] were given **but give [them] preference** over themselves, even though they are in privation. And whoever is protected from the stinginess of his soul—it is those who will be the successful.*

Surah al-Ḥashr: 9

Allah (s.w.t.) said in the Qur'an, *ithar* means preference to others; to your brothers and sisters over yourself, despite the fact that you are in need. *Ithar* is a very important quality that we have to teach our children, and the mother is the best one to bring this understanding to our children.

There is a *hadith* narrated by Anas ibn Malik. One day, the mother of the believers, Aishah (r.a.) hosted a poor woman. She walked in with her two daughters. Aishah (r.a.) did not have anything to give her but three dates. So the mother gave each child one date. While she was going to put the third one in her mouth to eat it, she noticed that the two girls were asking for the date, so she split it between them and she gave each one a half. Aishah (r.a.) was so amazed. When the Prophet (s.a.w.) returned, she told him the story. So he (s.a.w.) said, "This woman will certainly enter heaven because of this simple practice." (Al-Adab Al-Mufrad 89) Therefore, manifesting *al-ithar* is while you are sitting on the dining table with your family, and your child wants a fried chicken while his brother or his sister wants the same thing. Instruct them to *al-ithar* and teach them the quality of *al-ithar*. Remember the great reward that you will get from Allah (s.w.t.) by explaining the ayat of Surah al-Ḥashr to your children, *inshā'Allāh*.

# To be forgiving

In the beginning, I mentioned peace does not mean weakness. It stands for strength and justice.

The Prophet (s.a.w.), one day, said to his companions, "A man who is an *Ahlul Jannah* will walk upon you right now; will enter from this door." Everybody was looking anxiously waiting for him. It was 'Abdullah ibn Salam. Say the next day, the same person, the same statement by the Prophet (s.a.w.) and the same person walked in and the same goes for the third day. So 'Abdullah ibn Amr ibn As; was a teenager. He thought that he had to figure out why this man was *Ahlul Jannah*. He made up a story and he stayed with 'Abdullah ibn Salam for three days. He did not observe any extraordinary *'ibadah*. So he confronted him with the fact that the Prophet (s.a.w.) said that he is an *Ahlul Jannah*. He said, "Why? What did you do?" He said, "As you have seen, my nephew, I do not do anything special." He continued, "But wait a minute—when I go to sleep, I forgive everyone. That will bring peace and tranquillity to the heart. When I go to sleep, I do not worry about revenge. I do not envy any Muslims. I love everybody. I wish well for every Muslim." Do you know what 'Abdullah ibn Amr ibn 'As said? "Well, that is the one which we cannot afford." (Musnad Aḥmad 12286) Yes, it is hard, but it is easier when you learn it at a young age, as the mother is reciting the *ruqyah* and *mu'awwidhatayn* upon her children before going to sleep. She should also have caught upon them a bit of story, something like the story of 'Abdullah ibn Salam or the story of the people of The Cave. The Qur'an is full of stories. Allah (s.w.t.) revealed the Qur'an to be an *'ibrah* and admonition.

# Raising children

You see, raising children is not only about making them an MD or a lawyer or a dentist, and that is it. I came across many families. The main focus and the most important thing that the parents worry about, particularly the mother, is secular education. I am not saying it is not important. It is, of course, of great importance. But while we are caught worrying about whether our children pass their examinations, what happened to the Qur'an? What happened to the sunnah? What happened to the *sirah*? They do not exist because there is no room. The children I met used to tell, "My mother says, 'If you're good at maths, you're good at everything and in everything.'" Just maths was her main focus. This is not it. We try to change this wrong understanding by saying that you should be good in everything and the person who is good with Allah, good in his relationship with Allah (s.w.t.), will excel in all other fields.

So, mothers, these are the three reminders for you. To first sow *iḥsan* and *muraqabah*, then to be selfless and prefer others over oneself even though they are in need, and to adopt *al-ʿafuww*, or be forgiving to others. These are not the only elements in raising a child, however, these are the three that are being forgotten by many parents nowadays.

To conclude, once again, let's raise our hands and make *du'a*:

وَٱلَّذِينَ يَقُولُونَ رَبَّنَا هَبْ لَنَا مِنْ أَزْوَٰجِنَا وَذُرِّيَّـٰتِنَا قُرَّةَ أَعْيُنٍ وَٱجْعَلْنَا لِلْمُتَّقِينَ إِمَامًا ﴿٧٤﴾

And those who say, "Our Lord, grant us from among our wives and offspring comfort to our eyes and make us a leader [i.e., example] for the righteous."

Surah al-Furqan: 74

*Āmīn.*

# Q&A

**Q. In today's time, can women have it all—a career as well as being a good mother, capable of producing a good child?**

A. One day, on National Public Radio (NPR) that was in Texas, I heard a very interesting interview with a working mother. The hosts were asking her, "How much do you make per hour?" She said an amount and then the hosts asked, "Do you have children?" She said, "Yes." "Where do you leave them?" "With the babysitter?" "How much do you pay?" She mentioned an amount that is equal to what she is paid for working. Now, she is just working to pay the babysitter. Can there be any babysitter on Earth or any person to replace the love, passion, care and warmth that the mother gave to her children? There have been cases where trusting a maid or a babysitter with the care of children has resulted in disasters. Our children are our motive to enter *Jannah*. Why would we give that up? I do have many priests who are my colleagues and friends. One of them is a very famous priest. Every time I see him I would ask him, "How are you? What's up? How are your children?" He had one daughter. He keeps saying, "Well, Muhammad, she's good until she's 14." Imagine a religious person is expecting the worst to come. We invest in our children. We give our entire life so that there will be a continuation of our legacy. Then why do many Muslim women think that it is a shame to stay at home? It is perfectly important to acquire a degree and to be professional, but if your children need you, then they should be given precedents. If you cannot combine both, that is perfectly fine, especially if the family is in need of the financial support of the mother. Or in some cases, many single mothers have to go and work. May Allah (s.w.t.) help them. But what if the father is well-off, making a good income and the family is not in need of further income? Why would the mother go out when she had two, three or four children, or even one, and neglect her child in order to prove herself—I have a profession. I have a career and I have colleagues and I have duties to do. Do you know that in the States they called the housewife—the house engineer? She is the best one to look after the house and the household, so somebody has to do it and the best one to do it is the wife. If there is no need for the wife to work for example, financial need to support the family, then she is more than welcome to stay at home. But if there is, then that is a different story.

**Q. A follow-up question: So now what does she do with the career that she has spent so much time studying?**

A. OK, that is a good question by the way. I am a pharmacologist by profession, I was an assistant professor of pharmacology. My career initially was teaching pharmacology and pharmacognosy. OK, so when I shifted and I studied *shari'ah* afterwards, and left my job at the university and all of that, at one point I regretted it. I wasted so many years studying biochemistry and pharmacology, but well, by Allah later on, I realised that it was the best for me. It is very important for religious scholars to be aware of science and maths and many other sciences. Basically, to be aware of what is going on. Not to be out of touch with reality. So a mother who is educated—a physician, a lawyer, a teacher can utilise this knowledge that she earned from her degree in upbringing her children in the right way. Of course, it makes all the difference between an educated mother and a mother who does not have a degree. Let's take the 'benefit-risk ratio' as in pharmacology or *al-Maṣaliḥ al-Mafasid* as in *Uṣul al-Fiqh*, the *maṣlaḥah* should be given precedence to the *mafsadah*. If we have two benefits, we give precedence to the greater one. So which one is greater: raising righteous children or going to work? OK? Once again, we are not saying that it is unlawful for a woman to work, we are saying it is permissible if she works in the proper field with the proper etiquette and whenever it is needed.

**Q. My question refers to when you said that parents sometimes tell their children to lie to the guests about them being home. How can we avoid this situation? Because if we disobey our parents, we get sins. And if we lie to our guests, we still get sin.**

A. Well, that means you do that. And very often it seems. This is a very good question. You see, I hope this is appealing to the parents, who sometimes forget that as much as they are watching their children, *they're* being watched by their children. You know, at what age do the kids imitate their parents in praying? It could be before two years. Seeing you pray, they would bring a prayer rug and sometimes they pray opposite to the *qiblah* and they make some funny movements, but they are imitating you. The best way of raising your children is by setting a role model. Do not talk a lot, rather act. So I hope the brother, our young brother right now is giving a *naṣīḥat* to the parents. The answer to your question is if whomsoever to do something that is haram, they should not obey. Even if it is a father or a mother or a teacher, because the Prophet (s.a.w.) said, no one should be obeyed on account of disobeying the creator, Allah (s.w.t.).

**Q.** **The children are growing up and passing through university, but before they enter life, what advice would you give them to learn about the *din*? Because we spend almost twenty years learning what we will use for the rest of our lives, for our livelihood. But what we should learn before we enter our lives about the *din*? What advice would you give the youth of today?**

A. The answer should be presented in a series of episodes, actually, because this is a very serious matter and when somebody comes up to me and says, "O' Shaykh, my son is 17 and he is doing this or that, or he does not pray." The first question I asked him or the first remark I make is: "It is too late." Because it is too late. Where have you been until the child reached that age? What have you been doing all this time? Look at the Prophet (s.a.w.), he has given us the method of raising our children so afterwards you do not have to worry about them. You put them anywhere and you don't have to worry about them. He (s.a.w.) said to teach your children the prayer at the age of 7. Comes along with the prayer—a package of the *din*. Once they start comprehending what *ibadah* is, and how their *salah* or fasting is performed, you need to explain to them the *maqasid* and the aims behind this *ibadah*. So that it will not be just some form or sort of ritual. A few days ago when I met someone who said, "I am a Muslim, but I never believed in God." *I am a Muslim, but I never believed in God.* "I would go with my parents to the *masjid* and during Ramadan, I fast and pray *tarawih*, the long prayer. But I never believed in God." Why? Because the prayer was just some sort of jumping jacks. Fasting is just a routine. So now we need to transfer our *ʿibadah* from the routine perspective to the *maqasid* perspective—why do we do that? What is the purpose behind it? *Alḥamdulillāh*, there are no hidden secrets in Islam. As much as you think your children are very intelligent— they need to study a third and fourth language. Why don't you think the same regarding religion? They also need to study the wisdom behind the *ahkam* so that when they reach this age, they are not just practising, but they also understand, so they can move on by themselves. Another thing is when someone sends his daughter alone to study in the West. Even if she is the *ḥafidhul Qurʾan*, he is throwing her into hell and says, "Don't get burned." Throw her in the middle of the ocean and say, "We're ordering her not to get wet." That is not possible. This is haram. This is not fair. So we have to examine where are you putting your children? How is the environment? Because brothers and sisters, peer pressure is great. Peer pressure is beyond resistance, so you have to have mercy on your children and think positively about what will save them in this life and in the hereafter. From AlHuda's life programme and the private consultations, I get a huge number of complaints. Wealthy families send their children abroad to study by themselves, they ended up not praying, or the girl will be taking off her hijab. *Wallāhi*, they end up abandoning the *dīn*. Leaving the *dīn* entirely. They graduate and get their degree, and simultaneously, they get out of the *dīn*. These children are not well-equipped. Allah (s.w.t.) says in verse 6 Surah at-Taḥrim:

يَـٰٓأَيُّهَا ٱلَّذِينَ ءَامَنُوا۟ قُوٓا۟ أَنفُسَكُمْ وَأَهْلِيكُمْ نَارًا وَقُودُهَا ٱلنَّاسُ وَٱلْحِجَارَةُ عَلَيْهَا مَلَـٰٓئِكَةٌ غِلَاظٌ شِدَادٌ لَّا يَعْصُونَ ٱللَّهَ مَآ أَمَرَهُمْ وَيَفْعَلُونَ مَا يُؤْمَرُونَ ۝

O' you who have believed, protect yourselves and your families from a Fire whose fuel is people and stones, over which are [appointed] angels, harsh and severe; they do not disobey Allah in what He commands them but do what they are commanded.

Allah (s.w.t.) puts a priority to protect yourself and your household, those who are under your guardianship by every possible and prescribed legal means.

**Q. I have grown-up kids and I did not educate them as you have outlined. Now I am learning. But my kids do not listen. How do I teach them now?**

A. OK. One day, a family invited me to speak to their teenage daughter in one of the states. The mother in front of me was trying to convince her they were of Arabic roots. The mother was trying to convince the daughter to learn how to read the Qur'an. And she says, "Honey, if you learn how to read in the *mushaf*—not memorise—if you know how to read, I will buy you a brand new Mercedes." And she still was not interested, because she has everything. Does it mean that we have to give it up, "It is too late; so never mind?" Abu Hurayrah (r.a.) came to the Prophet (s.a.w.), begging him to find a solution because his mother was a *mushrikah*. And she hated the Prophet (s.a.w.) the most. Every time Abu Hurayrah walks home, she would deliberately insult and curse the Prophet (s.a.w.), and that upset him so much, even though he loved his mother so much. But he hated what she was doing. He said, "O' Rasulullah, pray for my mother. May Allah guide her. I love her, but I hate what she does." The Prophet (s.a.w.) raised his hands and said "O' Allah, guide Abu Hurayrah's mother." He (s.a.w.) made the *du'a*'. Abu Hurayrah went home and his mother was taking a bath. She says, "Wait a minute. I'm undressed." When she stepped out, she said, "O' Abu Hurayrah, *ash-hadu anla ilāha illallāh, wa ash-hadu anna Muhammadar Rasūlullāh.*" A very important component that many of us are unaware of it. Even though it is sitting in front of us, which is *ad-duʿa'.* Now, the only solution you have is to make *duʿa',* because the child is already a grown-up. It is hard to control them or advise them, and this teenage girl gave me a lesson. When I sat with her in order to advise her and speak to her logically, she says, "Uncle, I want to tell you one thing." She showed me a few things. "Look, that was my parents before you come into our life. They were not religiously committed." The way the mother was dressed, *astaghfirullāh.* "So now all of a sudden it changes. Fine, that is their decision, but they cannot impose that change on us overnight." She was very logical. "I'm not willing to change that fast, that dramatic change won't happen to my life." Slowly and gradually. So what I am saying is to use the power of the *duʿa'.* It is the sharpest weapon. Invite eloquent scholars and speakers to your house who can relate to your children. Bring them to functions like that so that they know that the *shuyukh* or the scholars are educated, they excelled in different fields, many from our doctors, many of whom are engineers, many from our artists. They are very, very eloquent and intelligent as well. Make them love the *din.* Take them for *ḥajj* and *ʿumrah*, but take them during the off-season, please. I mean it will be best if you can take them at a time when it is not very crowded so that they would enjoy the environment, enjoy the scenery, enjoy seeing the Kaʿbah and perform the *tawaf*. This is also one of the solutions and when you drink from *zamzam* water, ask your children to make *duʿaʾ*. Just ask them. You say, "You yourself make the *duʿaʾ*: 'May Allah guide me and open my heart to the truth'". May Allah guide all of our children. *Āmīn*.

**Q. What happens if we don't respect our parents? (This was asked by a young boy.)**

A. Bad things will happen. Very, very bad things will happen. Young boy, do you want to go to heaven? Do you want to play PlayStation in heaven? OK, in order to go to heaven there is only one way. It is to obey and respect your parents. Can we imagine the absence of the mother in our life? How important is her presence? I believe that any success I have in my life is because of the blessings of the *du'a'* of my parents. Do you want to be successful at school? Your parents have to be happy with you. If you want to be successful in your business when you grow up, you have to obey your parents. The consequences of disobeying and dishonouring the parents are awful. The Prophet (s.a.w.) counted the second major sin amongst the disruptive sins after disbelief in Allah (s.w.t.) is to be disobedient to parents. So, please be very careful if you want Allah (s.w.t.) to bless you. Once the Prophet (s.a.w.) was climbing the *mimbar*. And he said, "*Āmīn.*" at the first step. Then, "*Āmīn.*" at the second step. And "*Āmīn.*" at the third step. After he finished, the *saḥabah* asked, "O' Rasulullah, we heard you saying '*Āmīn. Āmīn. Āmīn.*' What was that all about?" He said, "Jibril (a.s.) came to me as I was climbing the *mimbar* and he made three invocations so he ordered me to say '*Āmīn.*' which means 'O' Allah accept.'" One of these invocations, my dear boy, 'O'Allah. Disgrace and humiliate the one who will witness the life of his parents or one of them and does not go to *Jannah* through them by being obedient to them and honouring them.' So there is only one way that you can go to *Jannah* after believing in Allah (s.w.t.) and praying—obeying your parents.

# GLOSSARY

1.  adab: good manners

2.  aḥkam: rules

3.  akhirah: hereafter

4.  akhlaq: Islamic ethics

5.  al-Munafiqun: the hypocrites

6.  amanah: trustworthiness; honesty

7.  ayat: verse

8.  din: religion

9.  dunya: world

10. duʻaʾ: invocations

11. faqih: an Islamic jurist

12. fiqh: Islamic jurisprudence

13. ḥadith: sayings of the Prophet (s.a.w.)

14. ḥafidhul Qurʾan: the Qurʾan memoriser

15. ḥajj: the major pilgrimage to Makkah

16. ḥijrah: the migration journey of the Prophet (s.a.w.) and his followers from Makkah to Madinah

17. iḥram: a sacred state which a Muslim must enter in order to perform the major pilgrimage or the minor pilgrimage; a specific attire Muslims have to wear for the major or minor pilgrimage

18. iḥsan: spiritual excellence

19. iman: faith

20. Islam: submission to the will of Allah (s.w.t.)

21. ithar: preference for others over oneself when in need

22. Jannah: heaven

23. madrasah: a college for Islamic education

24. mafsadah: an attribute of the act whereby corruption or harm happens to the public or to individuals

25. maqaṣid: objectives

26. maṣlaḥah: benefit

27. mimbar: a short flight of steps used as a platform by an imam in a *masjid.*

28. muḥaddithin: the scholars of *hadith*

29. muraqabah: meditation; to sit in solitude for some time daily and take account of one's own self and to see what mistakes one has committed

30. mushaf: a collection of sheets; a written copy of the Qur'an

31. mushrikah: a polytheist

32. mu'awwidhatayn: Verse of Refuge; the last two chapters of the Qur'an

33. naṣiḥat: advice

34. qiblah: direction towards the Ka'bah in the Sacred Mosque in Makkah, which is used by Muslims in various religious contexts, particularly the direction of prostration for the prayer

35. ruqyah: the practice of treating illnesses through Qur'anic *ayat*, and invocations prescribed by the Prophet (s.a.w.)

36. ṣaḥabah: companions of the Prophet (s.a.w.), who lived alongside him

37. shari'ah: law

38. shuyukh: scholars

39. sirah: prophetic biography

40. taḥnik: putting something sweet such as dates, in the infant's mouth after the birth

41. taqwa: piety, fear of God

42. Ummahatul Mu'minin: Mothers of the Believers; the Prophet's (s.a.w.) wives

43. ummah: the Muslim community

44. 'afuww: forgiving

45. 'atiyyah: a precious gift

46. 'ibadah: worship

47. 'Ibadurraḥman: the faithful servant of Allah (s.w.t.)

48. 'ibrah: lessons

49. 'umrah: minor pilgrimage to Makkah

# NOTES